Published in the United States of America by Cherry Lake Publishing
Ann Arbor, Michigan
www.cherrylakepublishing.com

Reading Adviser: Marla Conn MS, Ed., Literacy specialist, Read-Ability, Inc.
Book Design: Jennifer Wahi
Illustrator: Jeff Bane

Photo Credits: © Monkey Business Images / Shutterstock.com, 5; © didesign021 / Shutterstock.com, 7; © Burlingham / Shutterstock.com, 9; © Lolostock / Shutterstock.com, 11; © Toa55 / Shutterstock.com, 13; © JPC-PROD / Shutterstock.com, 15; © A and N photography / Shutterstock.com, 17; © Oleksandr Liesnoi / Shutterstock.com, 19; © Pressmaster / Shutterstock.com, 21; © Mediaphotos / Shutterstock.com, 23; © aleksandr-mansurov-ru, 2-3, 24; Cover, 1, 6, 16, 20, Jeff Bane

Copyright ©2018 by Cherry Lake Publishing
All rights reserved. No part of this book may be reproduced or utilized in any form or by any means without written permission from the publisher.

Library of Congress Cataloging-in-Publication Data

Names: Bell, Samantha, author.
Title: Doctor / Samantha Bell.
Description: Ann Arbor, MI : Cherry Lake Publishing, [2017] | Series: My friendly neighborhood | Audience: K to grade 3.
Identifiers: LCCN 2016056587| ISBN 9781634728294 (hardcover) | ISBN 9781534100077 (pbk.) | ISBN 9781634729185 (pdf) | ISBN 9781534100961 (hosted ebook)
Subjects: LCSH: Physicians--Juvenile literature.
Classification: LCC R690 .B3768 2017 | DDC 610.69/5--dc23
LC record available at https://lccn.loc.gov/2016056587

Printed in the United States of America
Corporate Graphics

table of contents

Neighborhood Helper 4

Glossary 24

Index 24

About the author: Samantha Bell has written and illustrated over 60 books for children. She lives in South Carolina with her family and pets. She is very thankful for the helpers in her community.

About the illustrator: Jeff Bane and his two business partners own a studio along the American River in Folsom, California, home of the 1849 Gold Rush. When Jeff's not sketching or illustrating for clients, he's either swimming or kayaking in the river to relax.

neighborhood helper

People visit the doctor to make sure they are well.

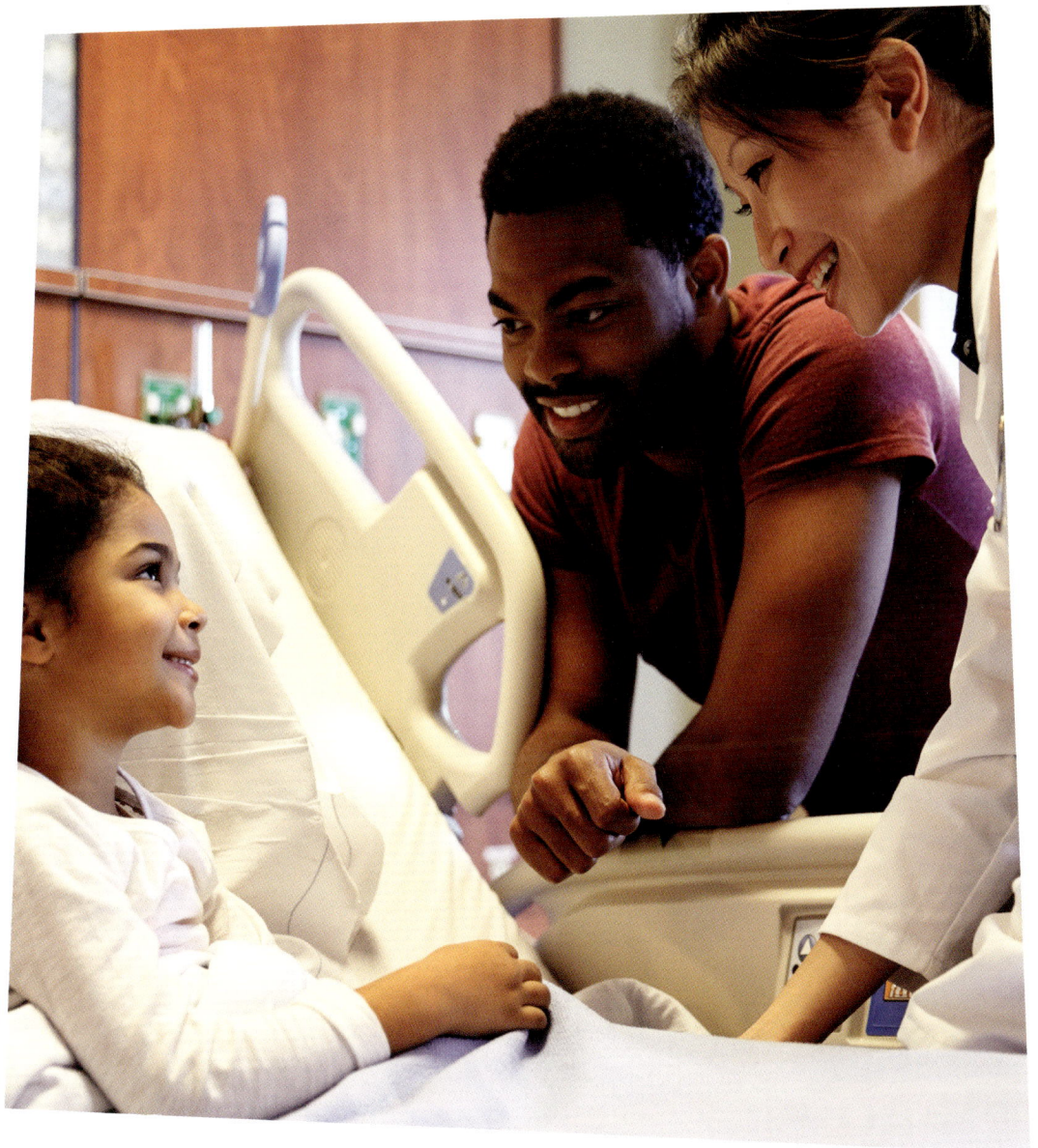

Sometimes people get shots.
The shots help people from getting sick.

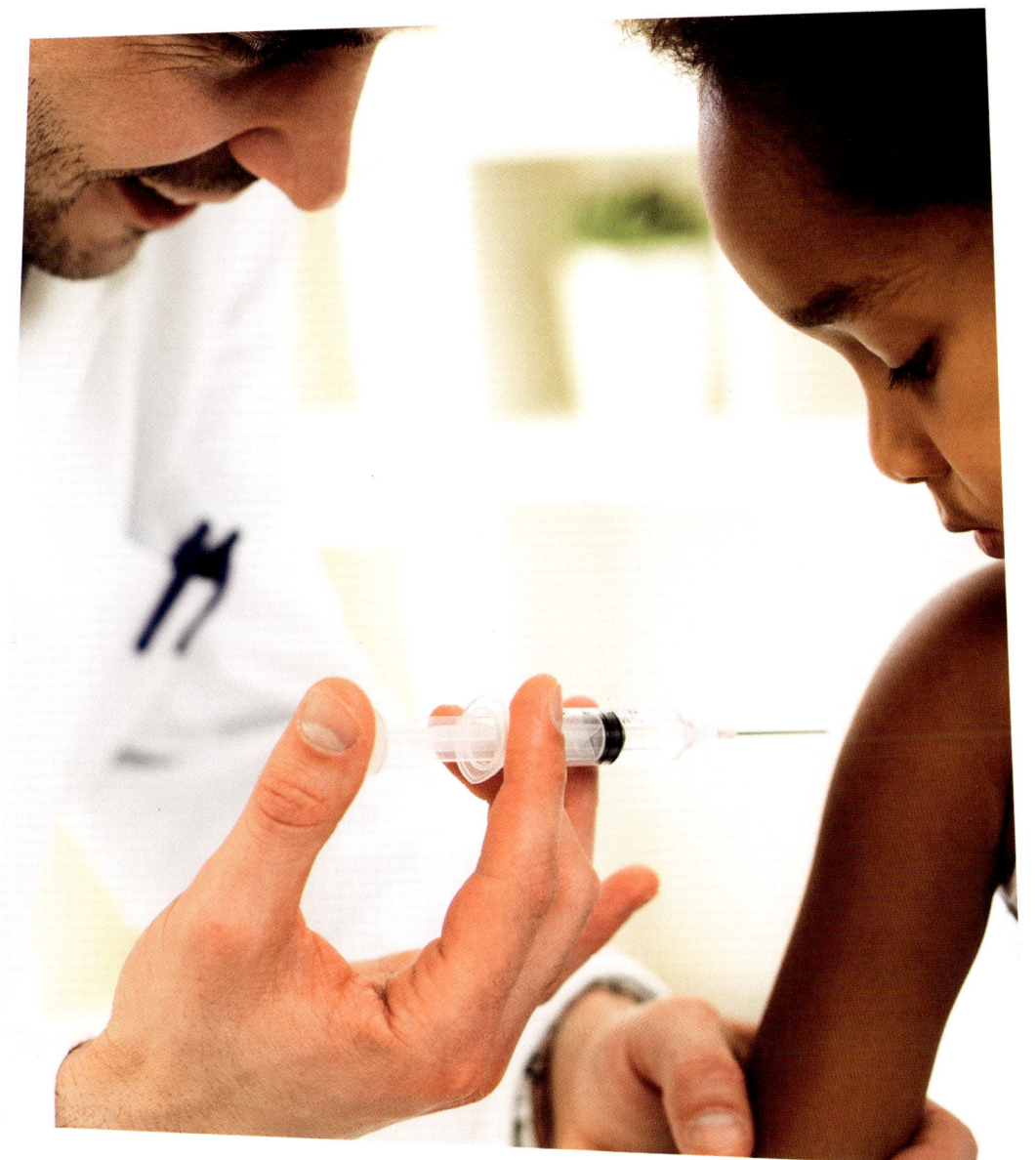

Doctors know about **medicine**.
They tell people what kind to take.

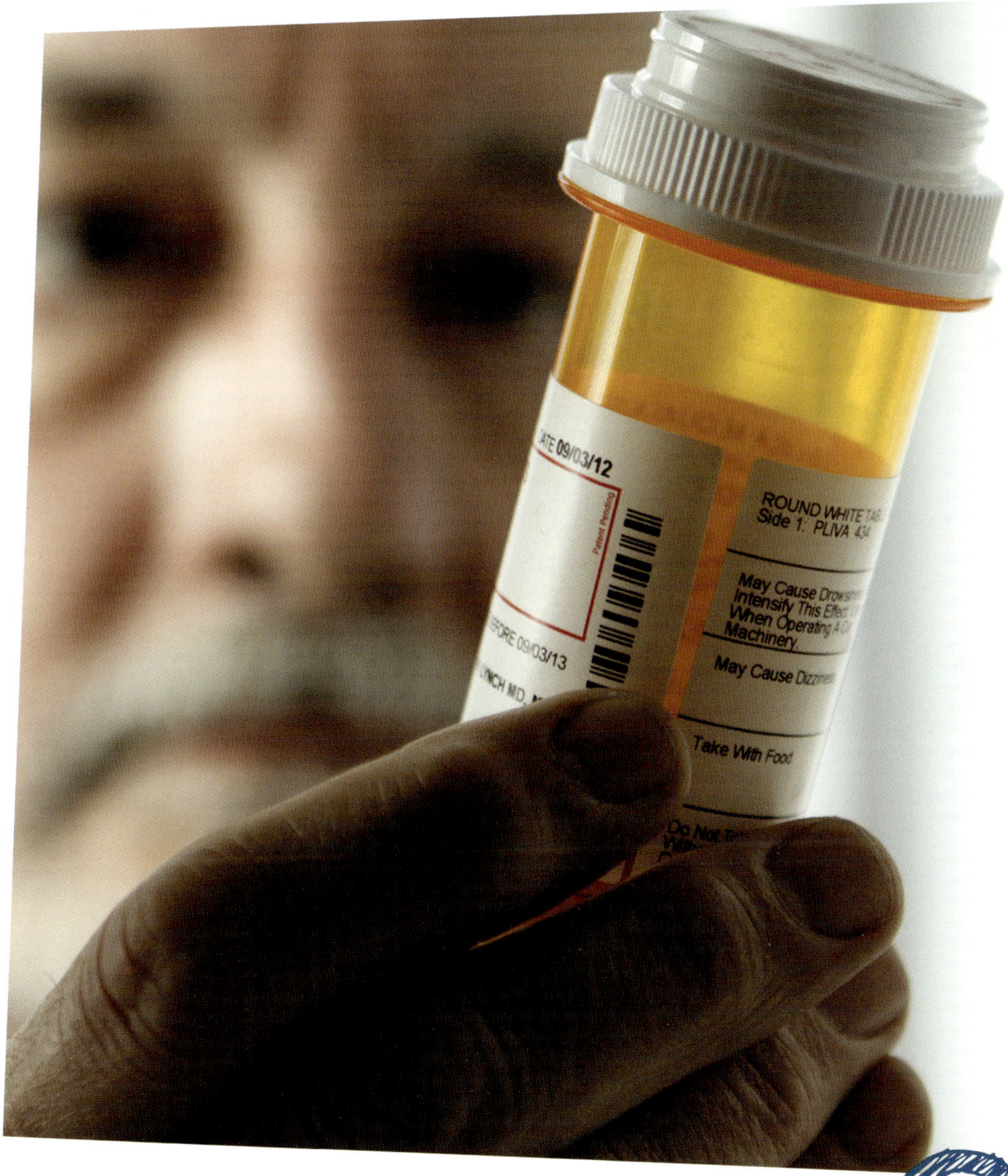

When did you go to the doctor?

There are many kinds of doctors.

Some **deliver** babies.

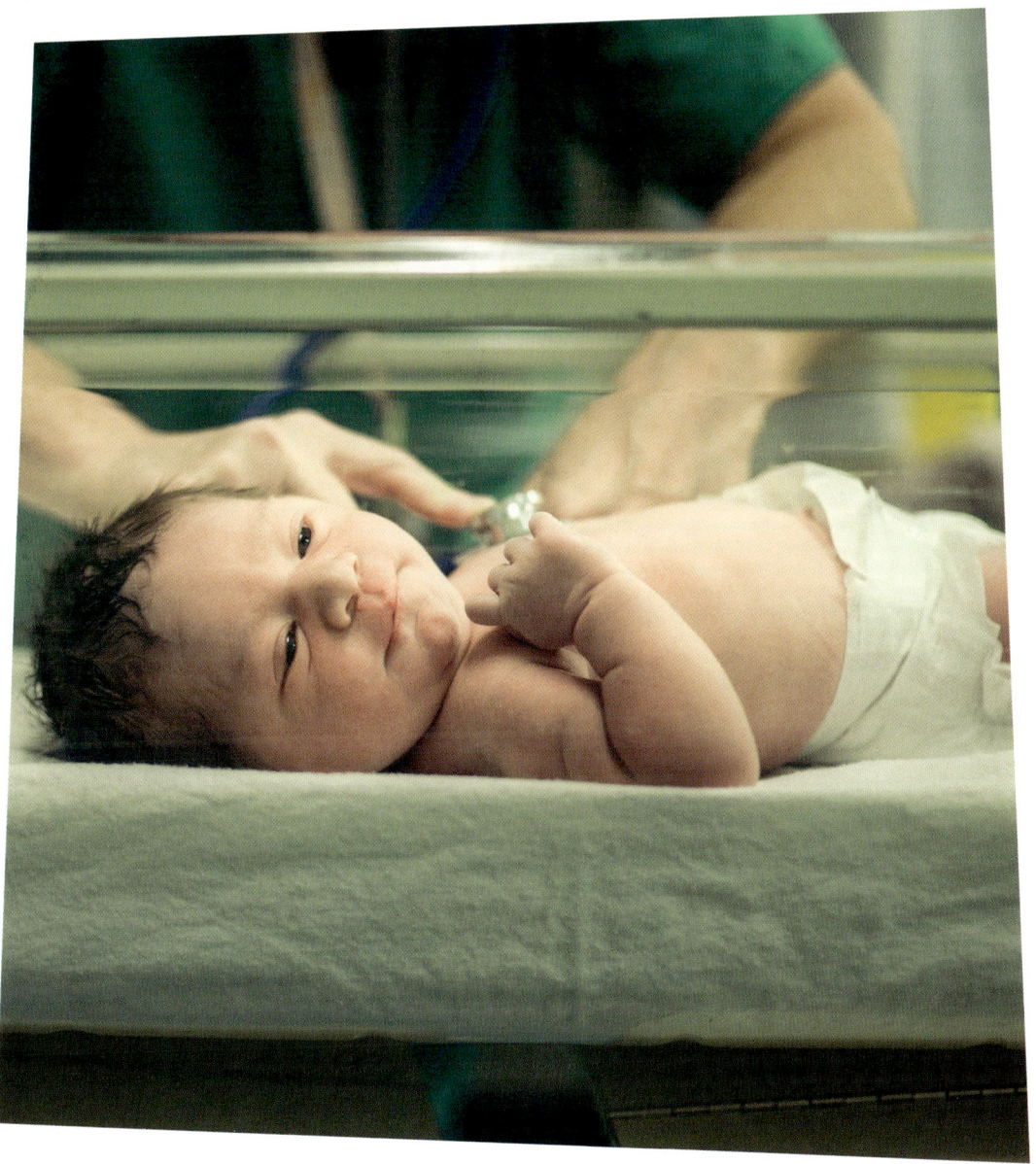

Some doctors fix broken bones.

Some doctors make sure children are healthy.

What is your doctor's name?

Some doctors are **experts**. They know more about one part of the body.

Some help the brain. Some help the skin.

Some work in the **emergency** room. They help right away.

Some work in a **lab**. They make new kinds of medicine.

Doctors keep learning new things. They take classes. They read books.

Doctors take care of us.

What would you like to ask a doctor?

glossary

deliver (de-LIV-ur) to help in the birth of a baby

emergency (ih-MUR-juhn-see) a sudden problem that requires help right away

experts (EK-spurts) people with special skill or knowledge

lab (LAB) a place for making scientific experiments and tests

medicine (MED-ih-sin) helpful drugs used to treat illnesses

index

bones, 12

fix, 12

healthy, 14

medicine, 8, 20

sick, 6

shots, 6